This book belongs to

_____

Dedicated to our daughters Ava and Mila who inspired us to write this story.

The day is here, the sun is shining, the **BIG BIG** world is waiting for you...

We wash our hands, we wear a mask...

and we stay far away.

We wear a mask when we go outside...

Mommy wears a mask...
Daddy wears a mask...
and I wear a mask

We play outside in our little **bubble**...

Bye Bye Rona

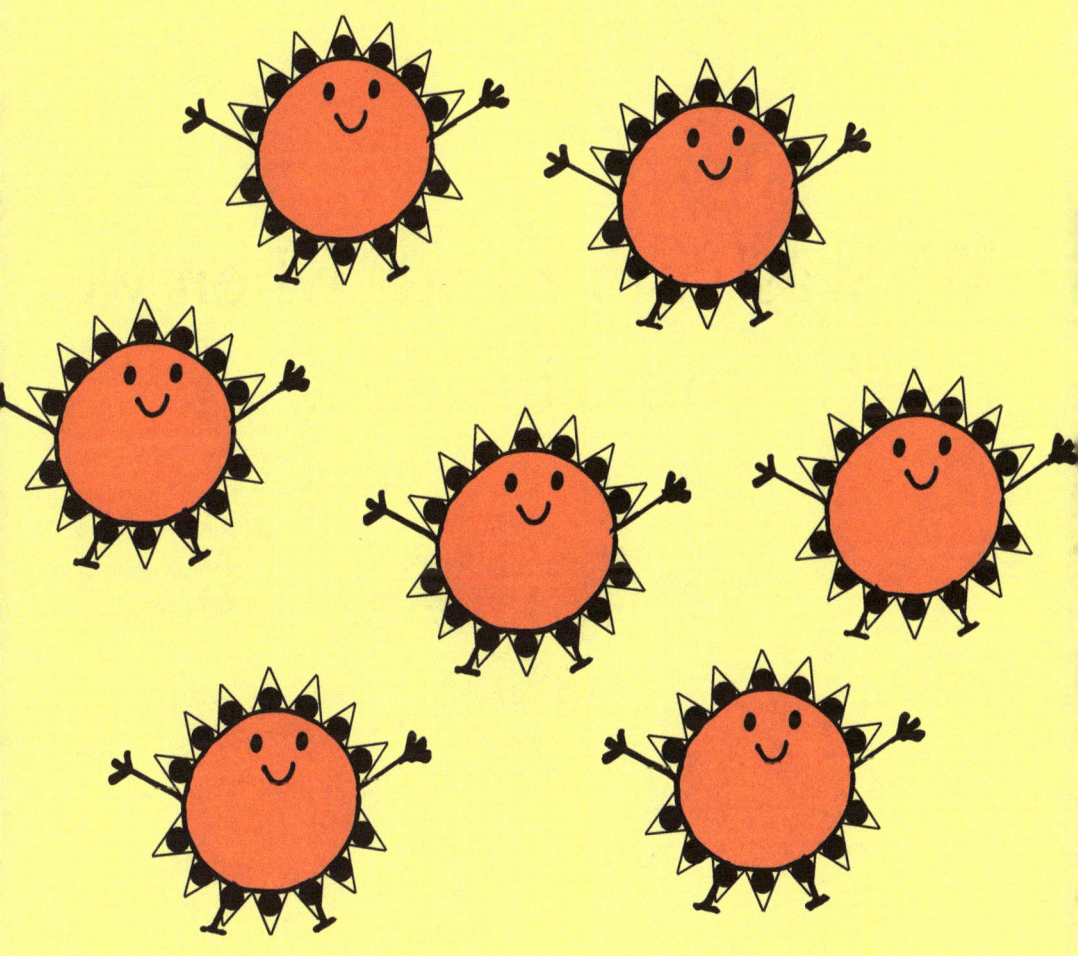

We wash our hands when we come inside...

Mommy washes her hands
Daddy washes his hands
and I wash my hands.

We do our part to stay safe everyday...

so we can stay healthy and keep **Rona** away!

It won't be long until we can explore...

Bye Bye Rona